THE G.I. SERIES

The Men of the Mighty Eighth
The U.S Eighth Air Force, 1942–1945

General Carl Spaatz, commander of all U.S. Air Forces in England, is wearing the winter service jacket. This was made from wool elastique material and was privately purchased. All U.S. officers, regardless of their branch, wore this jacket. Spaatz has the U.S. Army Air Forces (AAF) insignia on his left shoulder.

THE ILLUSTRATED HISTORY OF THE AMERICAN SOLDIER, HIS UNIFORM AND HIS EQUIPMENT

The Men of the Mighty Eighth

The U.S. Eighth Air Force, 1942–1945

Christopher J. Anderson

Greenhill Books
LONDON

Stackpole Books
PENNSYLVANIA

*This book is dedicated to all of the men and women who served with
the Eighth Air Force from 1942 to 1945.*

The Men of the Mighty Eighth
first published 2001 by Greenhill Books, Lionel
Leventhal Limited, Park House, 1 Russell Gardens,
London NW11 9NN
www.greenhillbooks.com
and
Stackpole Books, 5067 Ritter Road, Mechanicsburg,
PA 17055, USA

British Library Cataloguing in Publication Data
Anderson, Christopher J.
The men of the Mighty Eighth : the U.S. Eighth Air
Force, 1942-1945. - (The G.I. series : the illustrated
history of the American soldier, his uniform and his
equipment ; v. 24)
1. United States. Army Air Forces. Air Force, 8th -
History 2. United States. Army Air Forces. Air Force,
8th - Uniforms 3. World War, 1939-1945 - Aerial
operations, American
I. Title
940.5'44973

ISBN 1-85367-453-2

Library of Congress Cataloging-in-Publication Data
Anderson, Christopher J.
The men of the mighty Eighth : The U.S. Eighth Air
Force, 1942-1945 / Christopher J. Anderson.
      p.   cm. — (The G.I. series; 24)
Includes bibliographical references.
ISBN 1-85367-453-2

1. World War, 1939-1945—Aerial operations,
American. 2. United States. Air Force. Air Force, 8th—
History. 3. World War, 1939-1945—Campaigns—
Western Front. I. Title. II. Series.
D790.A795 2001
940.54'5973—dc21   00-066199

***Visit www.greenhillbooks.com and access the
Cumulative Index to the G.I. Series***
More than 2,000 images have been published in the
G.I. Series, creating one of the most extensive
collections of images of the American soldier ever
assembled and available to the public. The unique
reference index, which can be easily accessed through
the Greenhill website, serves as a precise guide to
this wealth of images in the series.

All photographs in this book are courtesy of the U.S.
Air Force.

Front cover illustration: Captains Larry Roth (left) and
Wallace E. Merquardt (right) direct a B-24 to the
runway prior to take-off. Jeeps used for control
duties in the Eighth, like theirs, were frequently
painted in highly visible color schemes to ensure that
aircraft following behind could easily spot them. The
control jeep was responsible for ensuring that all
aircraft were in their proper place on the runway
before a mission.

Designed by David Gibbons, DAG Publications Ltd
Layout by Anthony A. Evans, DAG Publications Ltd
Printed in Hong Kong

THE MEN OF MIGHTY EIGHTH
THE U.S. EIGHTH AIR FORCE, 1942–1945

It was early June 1942 and a group of Royal Air Force officers and local dignitaries had gathered at Wycombe Abbey, a girls' school in High Wycombe, north of London, to join Brigadier General Ira Eaker in formally opening the school as the headquarters of the newly arrived Eighth Air Force. After some opening remarks, General Eaker, the Eighth's commander, stepped to the front of the crowd. A man of few words, Eaker announced, 'We won't do much talking until we've done more fighting. We hope that when we leave you'll be glad we came. Thank you.'

It was just six months after the Japanese attack on Pearl Harbor on December 7, 1941. Unprepared for the requirements of a global war, America was now involved in a crash program designed to build up its armed forces. All across the United States, factories and training centers were working around the clock. One of the principal areas of the country's mobilization efforts was in aircraft construction. In 1939 the Army Air Corps was just a tiny branch of the army, consisting of fewer than 23,000 personnel and little more than a dozen strategic bombers. Alarmed by the success of Axis bombers at the start of World War II, President Franklin D. Roosevelt demanded that the country rebuild its neglected aerial assets. As a result, the Army Air Forces (as the Army Air Corps was re-named in 1941) underwent an unprecedented increase in size and potency.

As industrial production mounted and aviation cadets were earning their wings, the Army Air Forces (AAF) were busy creating the units in which they would serve. Among the first of the new units was the Eighth Air Force, which officially came in to being on January 28, 1942, at Savannah, Georgia. For the first months, however, AAF commander Lieutenant General Henry H. 'Hap' Arnold, was forced to send what few aircraft were available to beleaguered forces in the Pacific Theater and the Eighth remained an air force in name only.

Early in 1942, ground elements of the Eighth Air Force began leaving the United States for Great Britain. The first two units, 689th Quartermaster Company and the 15th Bombardment Squadron (without planes) landed at Liverpool on May 11th. These two units were quickly followed by many more. One of the first tasks facing this force was the creation of the facilities necessary to support what planners hoped would eventually become a strategic bombing force of 200,000 men and 40 bomb groups. While the RAF could provide some facilities, the vast majority would have to be built from scratch. Eventually, the Eighth Air Force would operate from 58 different airfields from throughout the United Kingdom, with the majority being in East Anglia.

The first combat mission in which Eighth Air Force crewmen participated was a bombing run against enemy airfields in Holland on July 4, 1942. This mission, however, was flown with RAF crews and in RAF planes. Two days later, a flight of C-47 transports marked the arrival of the first American aircraft in the United Kingdom. Throughout July and into August additional planes, including bombers, began to arrive at American air bases and, on August 17, 1942, twelve B-17 bombers led by Colonel Frank Armstrong conducted the first strategic bombing mission over occupied Europe.

Believing the defensive capabilities of the Boeing B-17 Flying Fortress and Consolidated B-24 Liberators would enable them to fend off enemy fighter attacks, Colonel Armstrong's mission, like all subsequent Eighth Air Force bombing missions, was flown during daylight. AAF leaders believed that only in daylight could they take advantage of the Norden bombsight, which was intended to provide bombardiers with the ability to hit enemy targets with pinpoint accuracy. Initially, there was a good deal of disagreement between American and British officers over whether daylight or nighttime bombing missions would be most effective for the Americans.

Mounting losses among American aircrews during the remaining months of 1942 and poor results had convinced many in the RAF that daylight bombing would not work and should cease. Soon, RAF leaders were demanding that American bombers cease their daylight attacks and join the RAF nighttime bombing campaign. During the Casablanca conference in January 1943, British Prime Minister Winston S. Churchill had convinced President Roosevelt to suspend daylight operations. Only the last-minute appeal of Eaker, who pointed out to Churchill that a continuation of the current strategy would allow the Allies to mount a 'round the clock' bombing campaign against Germany, ensured the survival of America's daylight bombing efforts.

At the time of the Eighth's combat debut the Battle of the North Atlantic was raging. Hoping to reduce the number of ships being lost to U-boats, Allied leaders ordered that many of the bomber missions during 1942 and into 1943 were to be carried out against German submarine pens and manufacturing facilities. The mission against the U-boat construction yards at Wilhelmshaven on January 27, 1943, marked the first American bombing of a target in Germany. Subsequent raids, with ever increasing numbers of bombers, were carried out during the early months of 1943. While these missions provided valuable lessons for the bomber crews and fighter pilots, the stepped-up tempo of operations and the high casualty rates meant that morale among many of the crewmen began to suffer. In an effort to restore morale, aviation surgeons recommended that a combat tour be limited to a fixed number of missions.

General Eaker agreed with the recommendation and in early March established the limit for combat missions at twenty-five for bomber crews and 150 for fighter pilots. However, although their combat tour was finished after flying twenty-five missions (later raised to thirty-five in August 1944), the casualties among aircrews were so high that until Sergeant Michael Roscovich became the first man to attain this goal late in March, many of the beleaguered crewmen believed that surviving twenty-five missions was an impossibility.

Despite the odds against them (in 1943 the crew survival rate was believed to be no more than twenty missions) the crews continued to board their aircraft and fly against enemy targets. One reason for the continued resilience of the G.I.s of the Eighth was the close-knit nature of a bomber's crew. The ten-man crew of a B-17 or B-24, consisting of tail gunner, two waist gunners, ball turret gunner, radio operator, engineer, pilot, co-pilot, bombardier and navigator, was a well coordinated team that relied on maximum cooperation from all of its members. The crews would spend time with each other off duty as well as during missions. The bonds that formed among crewmembers ensured that the bombers would continue to take to the air despite the losses. During the course of the war, no Eighth Air Force bomber formation was ever turned back due to a failure of morale.

The ability to maintain the morale of aircrews continued to be important as the tempo of operations increased considerably in the spring of 1943. During the previous winter, results had continued to be disappointing and people began to question whether it was worthwhile maintaining a strategic force in England. Undaunted, the men of the Eighth persevered. With the improved spring weather and the arrival of additional aircraft from the United States, the Eighth mounted increasingly more severe raids on Germany. On May 14 during a mission against Kiel, Germany, and less than a year after the first combat missions, the Eighth was able to put 200 bombers into the sky.

As the Battle of the Atlantic wound down, Allied planners could, finally, begin to direct their efforts to a thorough attack on German industry. In January 1943, General Eaker issued his POINTBLANK directive, which called for the destruction of Germany's aircraft industry. No more than a catchy phrase in January, it gained substance by June when sufficient aircraft had reached the United Kingdom for the Americans and British to begin a genuine campaign of round the clock bombing. On June 22nd, 235 B-17s struck the synthetic rubber plants at Huls, and, beginning on July 24th, a series of raids that came to be known as 'Blitz Week' was launched at a variety of targets in Germany and Norway. During Blitz Week, the Eighth sent more than 300 bombers aloft. Of these 100 were destroyed.

The continued heavy casualties were caused, in part, by the inability of fighter escorts to accompany the bombers all the way to the target. Throughout 1943 when the Eighth sent its bombers aloft, P-38s and P-47s would accompany the bombers as they headed toward Europe. Dubbed 'little friends' by the bomber crews, these fighters would protect the bomber formations from enemy fighters for as long as they could before running out of fuel. As soon as the fighters were forced to turn back, however, the bombers would have to engage in a running fight with enemy fighters all the way to their target. Then, after dropping their bombs and with some of their number often badly damaged, the bomber formations would have to fight their way back to the protection of their own fighters. Bombers forced to drop out of formation due to malfunction or damage during the period without fighter cover were quickly pounced on by German fighters and stood little chance of making it safely back to their bases.

The inability of the fighters to provide continuous air cover is one of the reasons that the August 17 mission against the ball-bearing and aviation plants at Schweinfurt and Regensburg was such a bloody affair. A huge undertaking, the mission called for one wave of bombers to strike Schweinfurt and then return to England while a second wave hit Regensburg and then traveled south to Allied bases in North Africa. Although it was one of the most intricate missions up to that point, casualties among the crews, particularly those headed to North Africa, were especially heavy. Of the twenty-one aircraft from the 100th Bomb Group who set out for Regensburg, only seven eventually reached the Allied airfield at Bertoux. Those formations that flew on to Schweinfurt suffered heavy casualties as well.

The participating formations were so battered that no other major missions were launched against targets in Germany until September 6, when 338 bombers were sent to drop bombs on targets around Stuttgart. Again, however, the mission deep into Germany without sufficient fighter protection was extremely costly. More than a third of the bombers launched were either destroyed or so badly damaged as to be beyond repair. Following the disastrous Stuttgart mission, the pace of operations slackened somewhat and many of the Eighth's bombers, accompanied by fighters, were involved in shorter, but still dangerous, missions attacking German V-weapons sites in France. Despite the heroic efforts of the ground crews to keep the bombers in the air, the mounting losses on deep penetration missions to Germany were threatening to unhinge the entire daylight-bombing offensive.

Some means of providing the bombers with protection to and from the target was now becoming a top priority. Although experiments with paper drop tanks had been successful, P-47s equipped with these disposable tanks could still only travel up to 475 miles into Germany. Aware of the range of the Allied fighter escorts, the Germans began the arduous but necessary process of moving their more sensitive production facilities further east. It was clear that if a means of providing long-range fighter escort were not found, it was unlikely that the bombers would be able to destroy, or even hold up, Germany's industrial capabilities.

A second mission to Schweinfurt, known to the crewmen as 'Black Thursday,' on October 14, was as disastrous as the first had been. Of 291 bombers sent to the target, sixty were destroyed and another 138 damaged. By the end of 1943, despite the tremendous production of American factories, the rate of losses being suffered by the Eighth was greater than the rate of replacements. The Eighth was literally flying itself to extinction.

Relief for battered aircrews finally arrived in January 1944 when the 357th fighter group, which was equipped with P-51B fighter aircraft, arrived in England and was assigned to the Eighth. Soon, additional P-51s began arriving. A superior fighter aircraft, the P-51 had a greater range than either the P-38 or P-47. Most importantly, with the addition of disposable, wing-mounted drop tanks, the P-51 pilots could accompany bombers up to 850 miles into enemy territory. This range allowed the bombers to travel as far as Vienna, well within range of the most important German manufacturing facilities, under the watchful eyes of the 'little friends.'

While there was much that gave aircrews cause for optimism at the start of 1944, many of the Eighth's members were saddened when, on January 5, General Eaker left the Eighth to command all Allied air forces in the Mediterranean. He was replaced by Lieutenant General Carl A. Spaatz, a close confidant of General Dwight D. Eisenhower, who was given command of the United States Strategic Air Forces (USSTAF) in Europe, which included the Eighth, Ninth and Fifteenth Air Forces. Spaatz's subordinate, Lieutenant General James H. Doolittle, was given direct command of the Eighth.

Under the direction of their new leadership, and taking advantage of the groundwork begun by General Eaker, the Eighth was finally beginning to operate at the level that had always been hoped for. Huge waves of American bombers bombed Germany by day and equally significant numbers of British bombers returned to Germany by night. The presence of fighter aircraft all the way to the target had dramatically altered the situation. In addition, by 1944, sufficient quantities of the improved B-17G, which featured a forward mounted chin turret, were beginning to arrive to replace the older B-17F and B-24D bombers.

Despite the improved aircraft and change of command, casualties remained heavy. A weeklong air campaign in February, known as 'Big Week,' resulted in the loss of 226 bombers. Unlike previous years, however, industrial production was able to replace those aircraft lost and although casualty rates remained high, the Eighth was able to put larger and larger formations of bombers into the air.

A milestone was reached during the first week of March 1944 when, for the first time in the war, American bombers were able to bomb Berlin. Although opposition over the German capital was fierce and casualties heavy, the week-long series of raids was a signal to the Allies that the Eighth had finally reached its full stride and a message to the Germans that nowhere was safe from the destructive power of waves of Allied bombers.

Working together, fighters and bombers continued to strike at the German aircraft industry until May 1944 when the focus of the Air Forces' missions was changed. Although raids on strategic targets in Germany would continue, from May until August, the Eighth was assigned to Supreme Headquarters Allied Expeditionary Forces (SHAEF). As a component of SHAEF, the fighters and bombers of the Eighth were ordered to isolate Normandy from the rest of the Reich in support of the D-Day landings. On June 6, the fighters and bombers of the Eighth flew more than 4,000 sorties over the invasion beaches and areas immediately inland, dropping more than 3,500 tons of bombs on enemy targets.

Following the Allied breakout from Normandy, the Eighth, now at its originally intended strength of 200,000 personnel and forty bomb groups, continued to support the advance of Allied armies across northwest Europe while at the same time beginning to strike at Germany's oil producing capabilities. In order to confuse German defenders and to strike at targets even further west, a series of shuttle missions were flown from England. Bombers on these missions were flown to targets deep inside Germany and then, rather than fighting their way back, continued east and landed at airfields inside the Soviet Union. As Allied armies continued their advance west, Allied bombers continued to batter targets throughout the Reich. By the summer of 1944, raids of 1,000 or more bombers were not uncommon.

Having secured complete domination of the air by 1945, Allied aircraft now flew at will. Although hindered by bad weather at the start of Hitler's Ardennes offensive, Eighth Air Force fighters and bombers, along with aircraft from the Ninth Air Force, played an important part in halting, and then turning back, the German advance. Meanwhile, huge formations of bombers pummeled German cities and factories including, on February 14-15, Dresden. It was during the controversial raid on Dresden that a firestorm begun by RAF bombers and added to by subsequent waves of American bombers

resulted in the destruction of most of the city and the deaths of tens of thousands of German civilians.

Unable to stop a single bomber formation, even with the assistance of a new generation of jet aircraft, the Germans were now suffering under an almost constant rain of Allied bombs. Almost nothing remained for the bombers to strike and the last Eighth Air Force bombing mission was flown by a B-17 and B-24 of the 482nd Bomb Group against Kiel, Germany, on April 29, 1945. The efforts of the men of the Eighth Air Force were then redirected to dropping badly needed food and medical supplies to starving civilians and former prisoners of war who were still waiting to be reached by Allied ground formations.

In just three years, the Eighth Air Force had grown from being an air force in name only to the most powerful air armada that the world had ever seen. During its time in England the aircraft of the Eighth had flown more than a million sorties, dropped more than a million tons of bombs against Nazi Germany and, with the exception of infantrymen, suffered the highest casualties of any branch of the Armed forces. Seventeen members of the Eighth Air Force received the Medal of Honor and 220 others had received the Distinguished Service Cross. Had he been present when the headquarters of the Eighth was officially transferred from High Wycombe, England, on July 15, 1945, to Okinawa, Japan, General Eaker would have been able to talk for a little longer than he had in June 1942. Within a year of the end of the war in Europe not a single Eighth Air Force aircraft remained in England, but there are many who today are still glad they came.

For Further Reading

Astor, Gerald, *The Mighty Eighth: The Air War in Europe as Told by the Men Who Fought It* (Dell Publishing, 1997).

Bowman, Martin W., *USAAF Handbook 1939-1945* (Stackpole Books, 1997).

Freeman, Roger A., *The Mighty Eighth: A History of the Units, Men and Machines of the US 8th Air Force* (Motor Books International, 1991).

Freeman, Roger A., *The Mighty Eighth War Diary* (Motor Books International, 1993).

Freeman, Roger A., *The Mighty Eighth War Manual* (Motor Books International, 1991).

Maguire, Jon A., *Gear Up!: Flight Clothing & Equipment of USAAF Airmen in World War II* (Schiffer Publishing, 1995).

Maguire, Jon A., *Silver Wings, Pinks & Greens: Uniforms, Wings & Insignia of USAAF Airmen in World War II* (Schiffer Publishing, 1994).

Right: Staff Sergeant Phillip Taylor poses for the camera. Taylor is wearing an A-2 flight jacket with a dark brown finish; earlier pattern jackets were commonly a russet shade. He also has a leather A-11 intermediate flight helmet, and an issue A-11 'hack' watch.

Below: A B-24 waist gunner peers from his position through AN-6530 aviator's goggles prior to takeoff. These were the most frequently worn American-manufactured flight goggles. Many members of the Eighth, however, preferred to wear Royal Air Force goggles.

Opposite page, top: Captain John Godfrey was credited with 18 aerial victories before being shot down in August 1944. Here he is wearing the officer's winter service jacket and 'crusher' cap. Having served in the Royal Canadian Air Force prior to America's entry into the war, he was authorized to wear the RCAF wings, visible on his right breast. Underneath these is the blue, gold-edged, Distinguished Unit Citation Ribbon. On his left breast, beneath his pilot's wings, are his other medal ribbons: (left to right) Distinguished Service Cross, Silver Star, Distinguished Flying Cross, Purple Heart, Air Medal and European Theater Ribbon. The Army Air Force wing and prop branch insignia is visible on his jacket lapel.

Left: Private Joe Binkle tends to his garden. Binkle is wearing the cotton poplin Parsons field jacket and the A-3 herringbone twill (HBT) mechanic's cap with the visor pushed back. Binkle has also been able to obtain a pair of Type D-1 flying goggles.

Above: A group of mechanics chat prior to the return of their bomber from a mission. The men are wearing a variety of HBT fatigue clothing. The sergeant (center) has stenciled his rank insignia on the sleeve of his one-piece utility uniform. Two of the men are sitting on empty .50-caliber ammunition boxes.

Above: Three officers trace the progress of their shuttle mission to Russia. Two of the officers are wearing khaki cotton officer's service shirts while the man in the center is wearing the wool gabardine A-4 flight suit over his service uniform. The weapon leaning against the basket is a Russian Mosin-Nagant carbine.

Left: Corporal James Mulhollen uses a Type C-2 wrecking truck to help salvage the wing from a damaged B-17. Mulhollen is wearing a wool knit Type A mechanic's sweater over his one-piece HBT coveralls.

First Lieutenant George Heilig signals the OK sign from the cockpit of bomber 'General Ike,' named after the Allied Supreme Commander. The bombs painted on the side signify each of the plane's missions. This B-17 has been left with a silver finish, but earlier models were painted in an olive drab camouflage scheme.

Left: General Curtis LeMay, pictured here after his transfer to the Pacific, commanded the Eighth's 3d Bomb Division from September 1943 to June 1944. LeMay was one of the Army Air Force's leading air power theorists. Here he wears the officer's cotton summer service shirt, trousers and cap. Officers in England often wore the summer service shirt under the winter service jacket.

Above: A flight of B-17Fs on their way to hit a target in Europe. This early B-17 is painted in the olive drab paint scheme. Later 'G' models of the B-17 featured a turret containing two additional .50-caliber machine guns under the nose, as it was found that German fighters favored head-on attacks.

Below: Wounded members of a 458th Bomb Group B-24 are evacuated. Each of the bomb groups in the Eighth Air Force had a different paint scheme on the tail of its bombers to aid identification during operations. A Dodge ambulance waits to take the wounded men to the base hospital. During 1942–43 the Eighth relied heavily on British-manufactured vehicles, and only began to receive American-built vehicles in large numbers in 1944.

Above: P-51 fighters were known to bomber crews as 'Little Friends' for their ability to protect vulnerable bomber formations from marauding German fighters. These P-51Ds belong to the 361st Fighter Group. The Eighth used the P-51D in greater numbers than any other fighter aircraft.

Below: Two ground crewmen, wearing shearling uniforms to ward off the cold, work on a P-51A in the early olive drab paint scheme. Although worthwhile fighter aircraft, the P-51A and B were unable to escort B-17 and B-24 bombers all the way to their targets in Germany early in the war. American aircrews suffered horrendous losses until 110-gallon drop tanks became available, greatly extending the range of the later P-51 models.

Above: The crew of a B-17 poses for a picture prior to a mission. Two of the men (standing second from right and kneeling first on the left) are wearing the F-2 electric flight suit jackets, which were lined with wires attached to a plug that could be inserted into the plane's electrical system to provide warmth during flight. The other crewmen are wearing a variety of bulkier jackets: (back row, left to right) a B-3, two B-10s and a parka-style B-9; (front row, left to right) a B-9 and two B-10s.

Right: A fighter pilot stands beside his P-47 before a mission. He has obtained a Royal Air Force (RAF) type C flight helmet with a pair of Mark VIII goggles. Members of the Eighth Air Force, particularly after it first arrived in England, used a wide variety of equipment supplied by the RAF.

Above: Pilots from 352 Fighter Squadron relax between operations. These officers wear a variety of gear, illustrating the casual nature of clothing worn during operations. The man seated at center has obtained a pair of RAF 1943 pattern escape flight boots. These featured leather bottoms with suede uppers that could be removed so the boots resembled black dress shoes.

Left: Pilots are briefed prior to a mission over occupied Europe. The briefing officer wears a blanket-lined winter combat jacket, commonly known as a 'tanker jacket.' This was popular among members of the Eighth Air Force, although seen more frequently in infantry units.

Above: Ground crewmen work on the engine of a P-47 'Thunderbolt' of the 78th Fighter Group at an airfield in England. The planes of the 78th were all painted with a black-and-white check design on their engine cowling. Squadrons within the group were identified by the color of their tail flap. All of the groups of the Eighth devised a variety of paint schemes to aid identification while in flight.

Left: Officers of a B-17 joke after a mission. The three men on the left wear the early B-3 'Mae West' life preserver. The B-3 featured a rubber flotation bladder enclosed in a cotton shell. On the front of the vest was a small leather patch designed to reduce friction from the parachute harness buckle.

887 PERPETUAL HELP!

312172
-F T

Top left: The crew of *Perpetual Help* is blessed prior to a mission. The crewmen kneeling on the right and second from the left are wearing the Quick Attachment Chest type (QAC) parachute harness. Unlike with other parachute harnesses, the parachute was not worn affixed to the QAC harness. Instead, when it became necessary to exit the aircraft, a crewman would clip his reserve chute (visible to the side of the man kneeling second from the left) to the harness.

Bottom left: Members of the 401st Bomb Group have an opportunity to look over a visiting P-51B 'Mustang' fighter plane. Several of these men have painted their planes' nicknames to the backs of their jackets. This was a common practice among aircrew and ground crew.

Below: The crew of *Button Nose* receives final instructions. The crewman standing at center is wearing a wool gabardine B-1 summer flying cap, popular among aircrew.

Top left: A squadron leader briefs his crew before a mission. The briefing is being conducted inside a Quonset hut, constructed of interlocking pieces of rounded steel. These huts were extraordinarily versatile and were used in a variety of roles by American forces during World War II.

Bottom left: Ground crewmen work on the B-17 *Delta Rebel*, an F model which lacked the chin-turret found on later B-17 models. The B-17F was the workhorse of the Eighth Air Force throughout 1943. It slowly began to be replaced by G models in 1944. Ground crews would work around the clock to prepare their aircraft for missions.

Above right: Captain Clark Gable explains one of the B-17's .50-caliber waist guns. Gable, a Hollywood movie star, volunteered for service in the Army Air Corps and made training films. Just visible at his wrist is the plug-in for an electrically heated suit. The open windows made the waist gunner's position extremely cold during flight.

Right: Ground personnel fill up a P-51D fighter from a 'gas wagon.' The P-51 had a tactical range of 325 miles without its external fuel tank. Once the fuel tank was added, however, P51s could escort bombers for up to 750 miles.

Above: Boxing legend Joe Louis (center) on a visit to an African American unit in England. Louis spent a great deal of time visiting Army Air Corps installations units throughout England. He is wearing a British battle dress jacket with his wool service shirt and trousers.

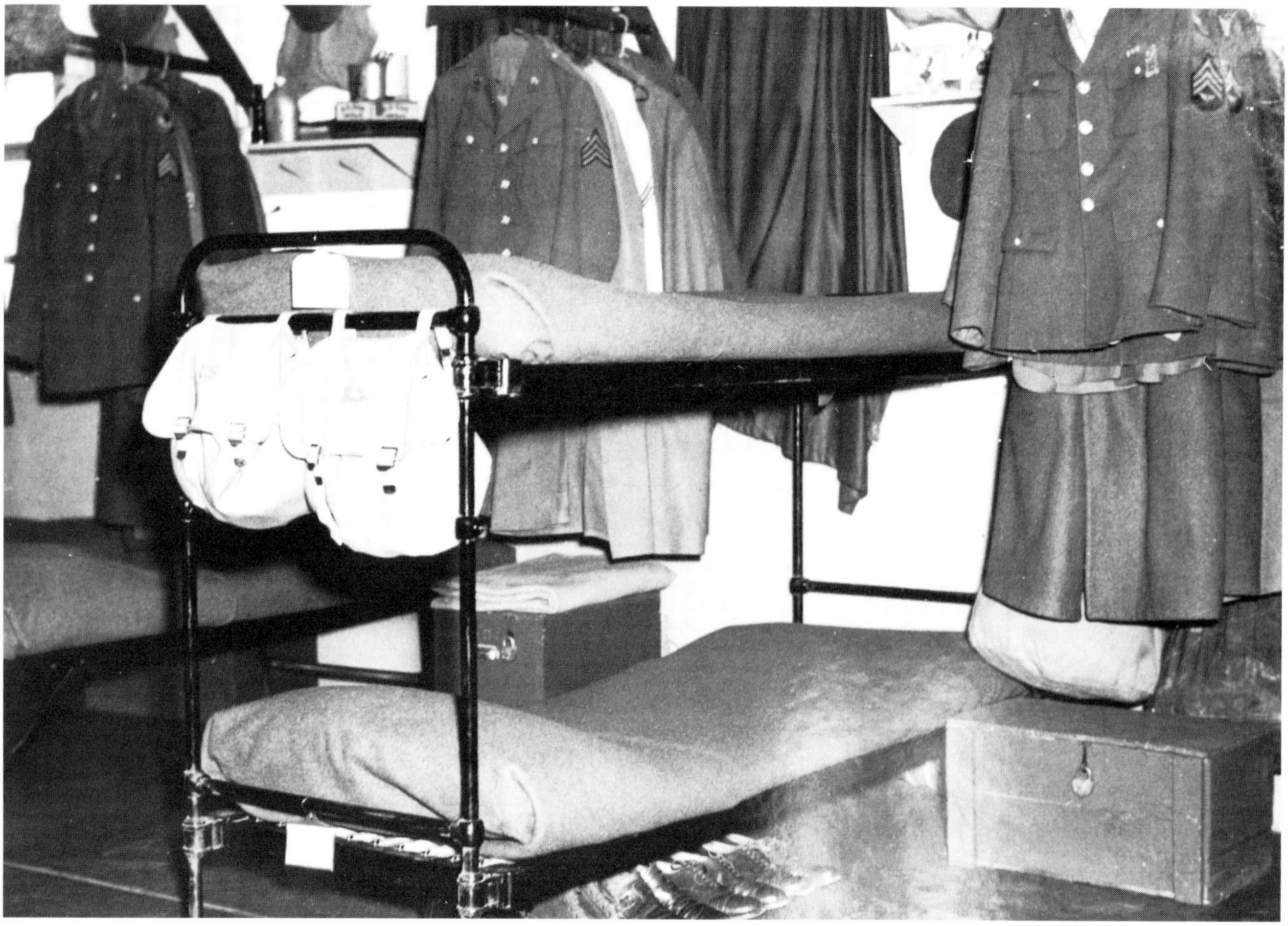

Above: Not all of the Eighth's bombers were B-17s. Here, a ground crew prepares a B-24D for a mission. The B-24 could carry a greater bomb load but could not fly as high or absorb the same amount of punishment as the B-17. The B-24Ds were used by the Eighth until May 1944.

Left: Enlisted barracks of the 303d Bomb Group, ready for inspection, October 1943. The clothing is all hung in a prescribed manner with the winter service jacket first. Just visible on the jacket at right are a pair of early Army Air Corps sergeant's stripes. These early chevrons featured a wing and prop insignia below the rockers.

Above: A mechanic works on a B-17 engine. He is wearing the cotton poplin Parsons field jacket, popularly known today as an M41 field jacket. He also has an A-3 herringbone twill (HBT) mechanic's cap. The A-3 was exclusive to the Army Air Forces and widely used by ground personnel. Many A-3 caps were stenciled with the AAF insignia, as was much other clothing.

Above: Ground crewmen work to extinguish a fire on board a damaged B-17. The large amount of fuel and ammunition on board a bomber, even after completing a mission, made firefighting an important, and extremely hazardous, duty for ground crews. Several of these firefighters are wearing Parsons field jackets.

Opposite page: A B-17 waist gunner keeps a sharp eye out for German fighters. He is wearing a B-3 shearling jacket with RAF type C Helmet, and a pair of shearling A-9 winter flying gloves. These were bulky, because of the extremely cold temperatures, but without them the gunner's hands would have stuck to his metal gun. Tight-fitting rayon gloves inserts were eventually developed for greater dexterity.

Right: Lieutenant Samuel Slaton signals 'bombs away' during a mission. The bomber formations' high-altitude flying meant that crewmen had to wear oxygen masks for much of their mission. Slaton is wearing an A-10A demand oxygen mask, which was used by Eighth Air Force crews in the fall of 1943.

Opposite page: Captain Fred Christensen was an ace credited with downing 22 enemy aircraft. He wears a B-8 back-type parachute over his Mae West and leather flight jacket. The D-ring for the parachute's ripcord is visible on the chest. If forced to bail out, the pilot would allow himself to fall free of his aircraft and then pull on the D-ring to deploy his chute.

Above: Brigadier General Leon W. Johnson (standing at right) talks to a crew that has just returned from a raid on Berlin. He is wearing an officer's trench coat. These popular coats were privately purchased and came in a variety of styles.

Right: Captain Burris blesses the crew of *Lonesome Polecat*. He is wearing a doeskin M1926 officer's short overcoat. These privately purchased coats, which came in a variety of materials, were often worn in preference to the longer, and heavier, officer's overcoats.

Opposite page, top: An officer presents awards to enlisted members of the 364th Fighter Group during a ceremony in England. The sergeants all wear the enlisted man's wool service jacket and trousers. All have Eighth Air Force insignia, which featured a yellow winged number eight on a blue circular field.

Opposite page, bottom: A young lieutenant of the 364th Fighter Group is decorated in July 1944. The lieutenant has pinned his pilot's wings over the sky blue combat crew patch. Although never officially authorized, the combat crew patch was widely worn by members of the Eighth who had flown combat missions. The AAF wing and prop branch insignia is visible on the lapels of both officers' coats.

Right: A sergeant from the 458th Bomb Group is congratulated after being awarded the Distinguished Flying Cross. He is wearing the winter service uniform and has his aircrew wings embroidered directly to his combat crew patch. His enlisted service cap has had its stiffener removed.

Below: Members of the 381st Bomb Group participate in a chemical warfare exercise. The man standing second from the left is wearing an M2A1 gas mask while the other three wear the M3, which featured a diaphragm allowing the wearer to speak more freely.

Above: Sergeant Wheeler of the 881st Chemical Company examines a British smoke generator that has just been installed on a bomber from the 381st Bomb Group. Wheeler is wearing the cotton field jacket and M1941 wool knit beanie cap. Many AAF ground personnel wore the A-4 mechanic's cap, which was similar to the beanie cap but did not have a visor.

Below: Chemical warfare specialists of the 91st Bomb Group practice disposing of a chemical bomb. These men are wearing special rubber-treated chemical warfare suits with M2A1 and M3 gas masks.

Right: Lieutenant Dunstan Abel, a navigator on *Fertile Myrtle*, paints a swastika on the nose of his plane indicating a destroyed enemy fighter. Each of the bombs above the swastika represents a mission. Abel is wearing the wool elastique service cap with the stiffener removed, which was permitted so that a headset could be worn more easily over the cap. The consequent well-worn appearance led to their being known as 'fifty-mission crush caps'.

Right: A radio operator examines the contents of a tool kit before his mission. He is wearing a B-3 jacket, B-6 helmet with RAF goggles, and RAF type D flight gloves, which were less bulky than the shearling gauntlets.

Above: A navigator charts his plane's course on a mission. He is wearing an HS-18 headset and, just visible around his neck, a T-30 throat microphone. His A-8B oxygen mask has a sack below the face mask that would inflate like a balloon as the wearer breathed.

Below: Two ground crewmen speak into a microphone during the first live radio telecast from an Eighth Air Force base to the United States. Such broadcasts were very popular with American radio audiences at home. The man at left is wearing a D-1 mechanic's jacket, which was similar to the B-3 flight jacket but was intended for ground crews who often had to work on aircraft outside during very cold weather.

A ground crewman offers refreshments after a mission. He is wearing a first pattern HBT jacket, which featured button cuffs and pleated breast pockets, over the top of a Red Cross sweater. Throughout the war, local branches of the Red Cross knitted a variety of garments, to patterns provided by the army, for use by the troops. This man has secured his watch through the buttonhole on his lapel.

Above: A Red Cross donut truck provides refreshments to Eighth Air Force ground crewmen. The Red Cross trucks were frequent visitors to airbases in England and were extremely popular, not only for their refreshments but also because their personnel tended to be young women. The photograph shows the wide variety of fatigue clothing worn by Eighth Air Force G.I.s.

Below: Officers enjoy a cup of coffee after a mission. On the right is Francis S. Gabreski, the Eighth's highest-scoring ace with 28 enemy aircraft destroyed. Gabreski is wearing a 'pink' garrison cap with black-and-gold officer's piping. Many Eighth Air Force officers wore these unauthorized caps.

Above: A group of enlisted men check into a Red Cross hotel in London. The Red Cross and YMCA provided low-cost accommodation to G.I.s on leave in several English cities. These men wear the wool service jacket. Two of them also wear the peaked wool service cap while two others have garrison caps. Peaked service caps were common among enlisted members of the Eighth Air Force, whereas ground forces rarely saw them.

Right: Aerial gunners practice their accuracy with an improvised skeet shooter. This shotgun stands on a .50-caliber machine gun mount. The gunner is wearing an A-2 jacket and wool service trousers. Although the A-2 did not provide sufficient warmth for high-altitude operations, many gunners obtained them for wear around the base.

Opposite page, top: A B-24 crew from the 44th Bomb Group poses for a picture. All of the men are wearing A-2 flight jackets. The man kneeling at the right has sewn his squadron insignia to the left breast of his jacket. Contrary to regulations, two of the enlisted men have not tucked their ties between the second and third button of their khaki cotton service shirts.

Opposite page, bottom: These B-24 crew members all wear RAF observer harnesses over their flight jackets. Simply punching the round box at the center would unfasten the harness. This feature was later adopted on many American parachute harnesses. As with QAC harnesses, if it became necessary to bail out of the plane, the crewman could snap his parachute to the clips on the front of the harness.

Above: The crew of *8 Ball* relaxes after a mission. The crewman on the left is wearing a complete shearling flying suit while his fellow crewmen are wearing A-2 jackets over A-4 flight suits. The crewman standing at the right is First Lieutenant Jack Mathias who posthumously received the Medal of Honor for his actions during a raid on Vegasack, Germany.

Left: Captain Robert Green (left) hangs on to his good luck scarf, a piece of camouflage parachute silk, while Captain Kent Hunt (center) tries to take it from him. Aircrew wore silk scarves to reduce chafing. They suffered horrendous casualties, and many crewmen adopted talismans they believed improved their chances of survival.

Below: Members of the 93d Bomb Group prepare for a mission. The photograph illustrates the various layers of clothing worn by aircrew members on a mission. The man bending at left is wearing a shearling suit over a leather A-2 jacket and A-4 flight suit. The man standing next to him is checking the fit of an M-1 steel helmet. Before the development of specially designed steel helmets, aircrew would wear the standard M-1 helmets that had been 'stretched' at special airfield workshops to fit over a flying helmet with bulging ear-phone housings.

Above: A crew lies in the sun and waits for the order to take off. The man at the front is wearing a B-3 flight jacket over a worsted wool type A V-neck mechanic's sweater. Unlike the ground forces sweater, the AAF V-neck had no button closure at the front. He is also wearing a one-piece HBT mechanic's coverall and cap toed service shoes.

Above: Captain Donald Gentile leaves the cockpit of his P-51 after a mission. Gentile was credited with twenty enemy aircraft destroyed. He is wearing an RAF pattern 1941 life-saving vest over his alpaca-lined cotton B-10 flight jacket. As one of the first American pilots in the European Theater of Operations (ETO), Gentile has also obtained a pair of 1941 pattern RAF flight gloves.

Opposite page, top: The crew of *Doolittle's Destroyer* boards the truck that will take it back to quarters after a mission. The B-17's gunners have removed their .50-caliber machine guns from their positions and will return them to their squadron ordnance officer for maintanence. Several of the crewmen around the truck are wearing shearling-lined A-6 flight boots.

Opposite page, bottom: Two crewmen load parachute harnesses and flak armor onto a jeep for transport to the flight line. The armored vests began to reach aircrews in October 1943 and were copied from similar British models. Although bulky, the vests provided some protection from enemy anti-aircraft fire. They were worn draped over the shoulders and could be shed by using a quick release tab at the front.

OOLITTLE'S
ESTROYER

X 25 1 S

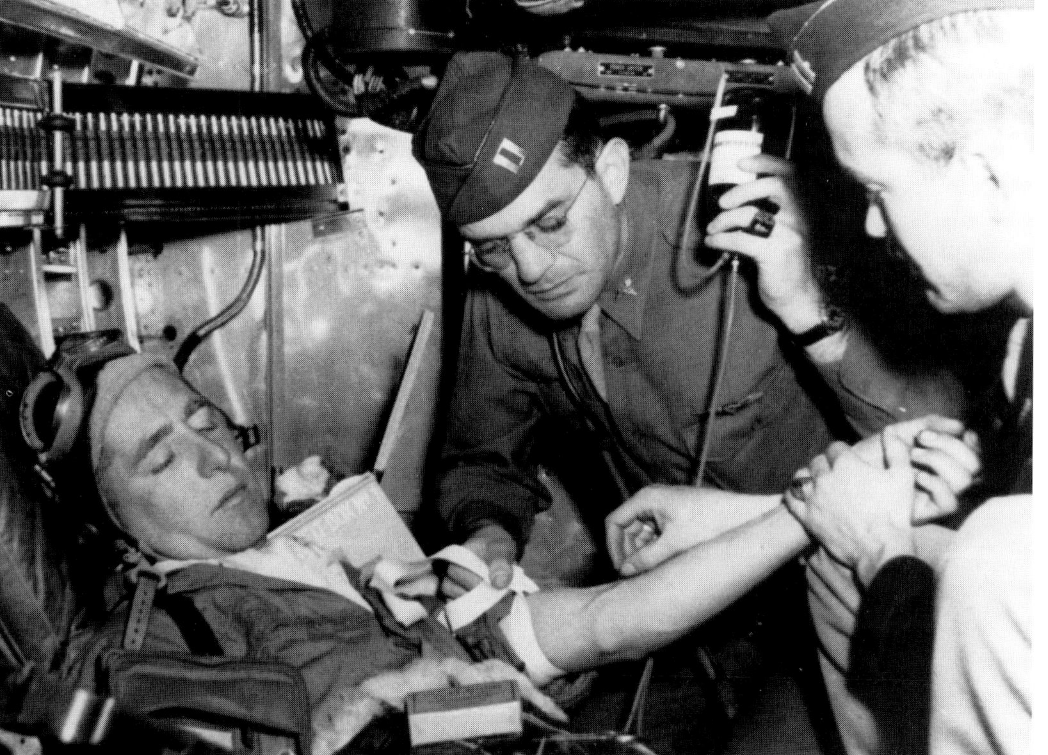

Above: A B-17 crew returns from a mission over Frankfurt. Two of th men are carrying their equipment in aviator's ki bags. The man walking second from the left has draped his flak vest over his left shoulder.

Left: Plasma is delivered to a wounded crewman. Injured crewmen could not receive adequate medical attention while o a mission and so medical personnel would be waiting on the runway to treat them immediately upon landing. The surgeon (center) is wearing medical insignia on the left collar of his officer's shirt. His flight surgeon's wings are visible on the left breast of his shirt.

Above: Members of the 1142 Military Police Company (Aviation) in March 1944. Military policemen were responsible for airfield security and a variety of other tasks. These men are all wearing wool service jackets and caps. They have tucked their trousers into M1938 pattern dismounted leggings. The dark blue-and-white MP brassard is worn slipped onto the left shoulder. The men also wear brown leather garrison belts and shoulder carriages. Although discontinued for general use in 1942, the garrison belt was worn by MPs throughout the war.

Below: Members of a choir from the 827th, 829th, 847th and 859th Aviation Engineer Battalions perform at an airbase in England. The aviation engineer battalions were crucial in constructing the infrastructure that the Eighth Air Force required to operate from England. All of these men are wearing winter service uniforms, and several have AAF branch insignia on the left shoulder of their jackets.

Right: A briefing for a mission. Two of the three men in the front row are wearing RAF goggles. The man at the left also has an RAF flight helmet. He is wearing a B-3 flight jacket over the top of an A-2 flight jacket. His shearling-lined A-9 winter gauntlets are draped over the machine gun in front of him.

Opposite page, top: General Johnson (center) briefs a crew prior to take-off. The man at left with his back to the camera is wearing an A-2 jacket that he has decorated with his plane's name. Just visible at his right wrist is the plug-in for an electric flight suit. The man next to him is wearing a B-8 parachute over a 1941 pattern RAF Sidcot flying suit.

Opposite page, bottom: First Lieutenant Manford Cory (left) explains his mission to Major Harry Downing. Cory is wearing an alpaca lined cotton B-10 jacket and a 'crusher' cap. Around his neck he is wearing a scarf of camouflage parachute fabric. Downing is wearing a B-15 jacket, which was similar to the B-10 but featured slash pockets instead of patch pockets at the front. The AAF insignia was stenciled to the left shoulder of most cotton flight jackets.

Left: B-24 crewmen study maps and intelligence information between missions. The G.I. seated second from the left is wearing a B-2 cap with the visor pushed up, a popular style. The models on the table behind the two seated men were used to brief the crews on formation flying.

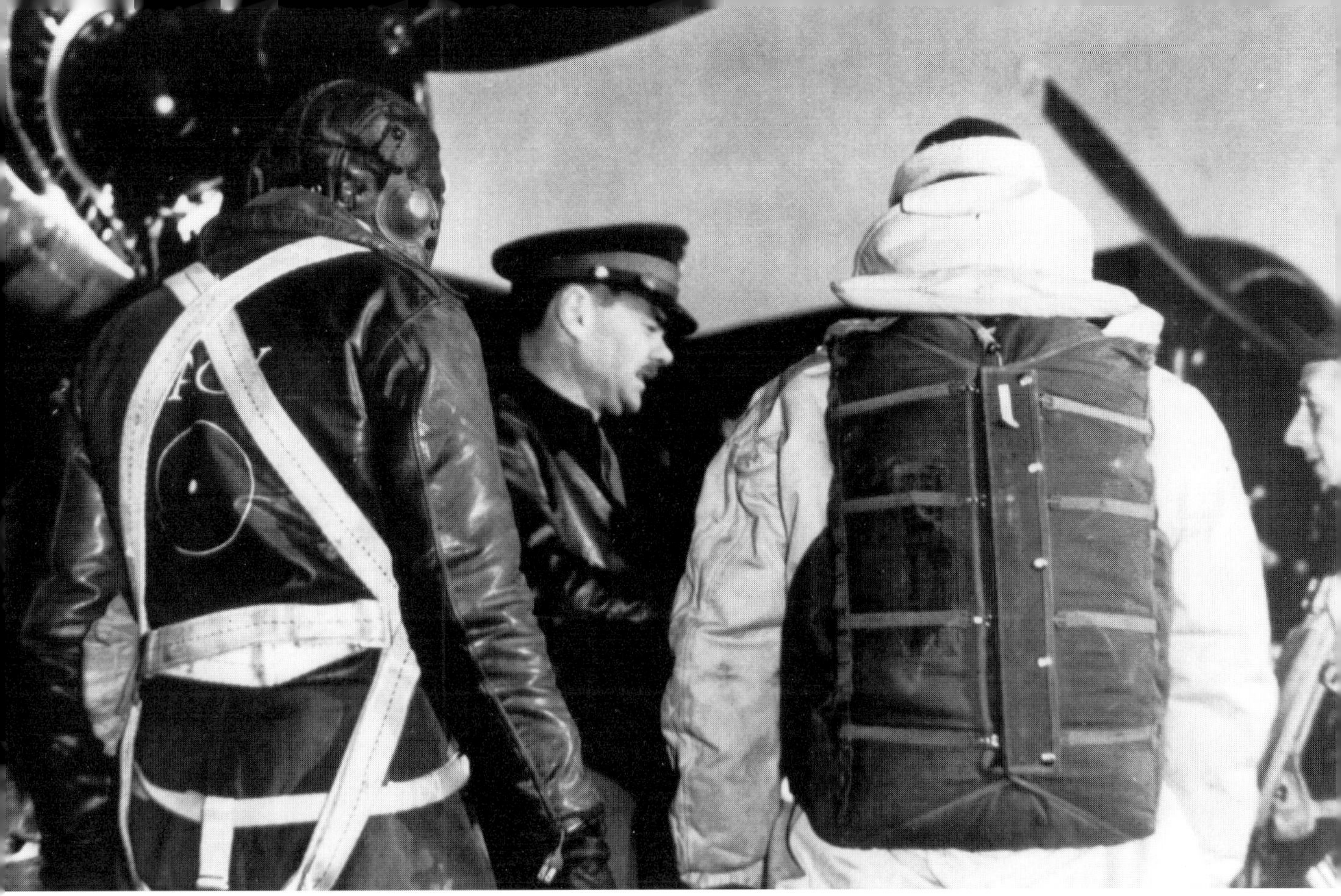

Opposite page, top: General Spaatz (second from left) and General Eaker (third from left) are briefed by a recently returned crew from the 303d Bomb Group. An upside-down M-3 flak helmet is visible on the table.

Right: Enlisted men line up in front of Quonset huts for pay call. An officer seated behind a blanket-covered table issues them their pay. The men are wearing a variety of fatigue clothing and the man at the front of the line has the cotton service shirt and trousers with HBT Daisy Mae fatigue hat.

Opposite page, bottom left: Two members of the 401st Bomb Group wait outside a mobile control tower to guide returning planes into their airfield. The man in the front is wearing the D-1 jacket while the G.I. behind him has a pair of B-1 shearling mechanic's trousers.

Opposite page, bottom right: A captain of the 401st Bomb Group scans the skies for returning bombers. He holds a Very pistol in his right hand. This fired flares to signal conditions on the airfield to returning crews. He is wearing the officer's winter service jacket with a British-manufactured Eighth Air Force insignia, identifiable by the 'stubby' wings, on the left shoulder.

Below: Members of the 381st Bomb group are interrogated after their first mission over enemy territory. The crewmen are all wearing A-2 jackets and several of the men have sewn leather nametapes to the left breast of their jackets.

Above left: A signalman flashes instructions to incoming aircraft. He is wearing an M1942 blanket-lined cotton poplin Mackinaw jacket and an HBT mechanic's cap. The T-30 throat microphone around his neck enables communication with the control tower.

Above right: Lieutenant William Lawrence, a bombardier, peers from his nose position. Lawrence is wearing an A-14 oxygen mask with AN-6530 goggles. Ammunition for Lawrence's .50-caliber machine gun hangs over his head.

Left: The bombardier of the B-17 *Hells Angels* looks over his equipment. He is wearing a B-5 winter flying helmet with RAF goggles. The connecting cord from his internal headset to the plane's intercom system is visible hanging down behind his right ear. His A-8 oxygen mask is visible around his neck.

Above: The crewmen of the B-17 *Chug-a-Lug* recount their recently concluded mission. They wear a variety of flight clothing. The officer standing third from the right has chosen to wear his F-2 electric suit over the rest of his flight clothing.

Below: A crew from the 753d Bomb Squadron poses in front of a B-24. The whole crew wears the cotton and alpaca flying clothing that began to reach the Eighth Air Force in large quantities in 1944, reflecting the more uniform late-war appearance of the typical bomber crew. All of the men except one have plastic B-8 flight goggles.

Above: A Red Cross worker, kneeling on the hood of the jeep, delivers coffee and donuts to members of the 91st Bomb Group's ordnance section. The crewmen are all wearing a variety of fatigue clothing including the one-piece HBT work suit and A-3 mechanic's caps. Others, including the two non commissioned officers (NCOs) seated on the left front fender, are wearing the wool service shirt and trousers. Most of these men are also wearing the cap-toed service shoe.

Left: G.I.s of the 353d Fighter Group enjoy a drink from their canteen cups at 'Ye O' Yankee Pub.' The sergeant at the right is wearing a second-pattern wool ETO jacket, which featured patch pockets, over his HBT work trousers. All of these men are wearing a variety of well-worn HBT fatigue uniforms. The man standing on the left is also wearing the cotton poplin field jacket.

Opposite page, bottom: A photographer is helped into a bomber for a mission over Europe. He wears shearling trousers and jacket, and has a pair of shearling-lined suede RAF 1940 pattern flight boots. These were very popular with Eighth Air Force personnel.

Above left: Two combat photographers discuss a close call after their latest mission. The photographer on the left is wearing the wool gabardine A-9 flight helmet. The A-9 was constructed of the same material as the A-4 flight suit, which both men are wearing.

Above right: An aerial photographer prepares his K-20 camera for use during an operation. Aerial photographs were a crucial part of all Eighth Air Force missions, allowing intelligence officers to assess damage to targets. This crewman is wearing a B-3 jacket and B-6 helmet. He has a pair of AN-6530 flight goggles on his helmet. The American-manufactured aluminum and glass AN-6530s were worn in conjunction with various RAF goggles throughout the war.

Left: Officers are debriefed after a mission. The officer leaning over the photographs second from the left is wearing the C-2 winter flying vest. The C-2 was a wool knit sweater closed with a slide fastener at the front. It was usually worn underneath additional layers of flight clothing.

Below: Captain Billy Southworth (right) discusses baseball with comedian Bob Hope. Southworth is wearing a tailor-made 'Ike' jacket, made from a cut-down winter service jacket. The stylish Eisenhower jacket was very popular with Eighth Air Force officers and men.

Below: Bomber crewmen enjoy coffee and donuts after a mission. The man standing on the left is wearing the gabardine A-9 flight helmet with a pair of RAF goggles. The crewman on the right wears a one-piece HBT utility uniform.

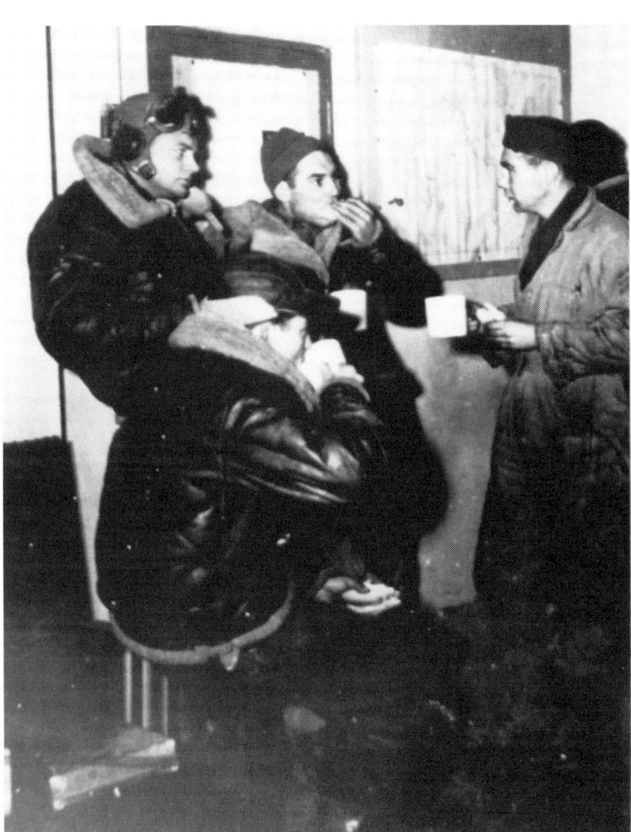

Above: An aircrew enjoys the company of two Red Cross workers after a mission. Squadron insignia are visible on the left breast of three of these men. The man seated left has stenciled his nickname to the underside of his B-2 cap's visor. This cap was frequently worn with the visor pushed back.

Right: First Lieutenant Robert Johnson relaxes with a game of chess. Johnson, a fighter pilot, had 28 victories by the end of the war. He is wearing the A-2 flight jacket with a white silk scarf.

Above: Pilots line up for a hot cup of coffee after a mission over Europe. Most wear the cotton B-10 flight jacket and crush caps. The pilot on the left, however, is wearing a winter combat jacket.

Below: Major Glenn Miller (seated center) enjoys a meal at an Eighth Air Force Base in England. Miller's famous AAF Band played frequently at air bases throughout England before its leader's untimely death in the summer of 1944. On the left shoulder of Miller's service dress jacket is the insignia for Supreme Headquarters Allied Expeditionary Forces (SHAEF), the command to which Miller was assigned.

Above: A Red Cross worker hands two bomber crewmen their reserve parachutes. These officers have bundled up to ward off the cold in their aircraft. Rather than wear shearling-lined flight boots, however, the officer on the left has chosen to wear the cotton and rubber arctic overshoes.

Right: Three gunners prepare to practice their accuracy on the skeet range. Skeet shooting served as a form of recreation and training. Two of the men are wearing wool enlisted garrison caps. Although these two caps lack piping, many enlisted service caps had AAF blue-and-orange branch of service piping.

Above: Officers and enlisted men from the 388th Bomb Group enjoy a drink. All of the enlisted men are wearing the winter service uniform while the officers wear 'pink' trousers with either a dark olive shirt (center) or cut down service jackets. The photograph illustrates the color differences between officer and enlisted uniforms.

Below: Members of the 401st Bomb Group's motor pool huddle around a small stove for warmth. Although they are in the ground crew, several of these men have obtained B-3 shearling flight jackets. The two men with pipes, however, are wearing the more common Parsons field jacket.

Right: Members of the 401st Bomb Group enjoy a drink at the sergeants' club. The sergeant on the left and the one second from the right have been able to obtain British battle dress jackets. The short British jacket was worn by many members of the Eighth, who believed that it was more fashionable, and comfortable, than the winter service jacket. In addition to his battle dress jacket, the sergeant on the right is also wearing a pair of moccasins. Use of such casual footwear is extremely unusual.

Below: Actress Marlene Dietrich visits members of the 401st Bomb Group. Two of the officers are wearing privately purchased jackets. The influence of the British battle dress jacket on the cut of their own uniforms is clear. The officer on the left is wearing 'green' jacket, shirt, trousers and garrison cap. His cap is piped in the black-and-gold insignia, which was the piping for all Army officers, except generals, regardless of branch.

Left: Sergeant James King prepares his camera for a mission. King is wearing an A-4 parachute harness over his A-2 jacket. If it became necessary to bail out, the parachute could be quickly attached to the clips on the harness. A first model airborne first aid kit, which featured a slide fastener closure, had been attached to the right shoulder of the harness.

Opposite page, top: Combat crewmen study a map of Europe. Two of them have decorated the back of their A-2 flight jackets with the nose art and name of their bomber. Flight jackets were painted by talented individuals at the unit level and were popular, although unofficial, alterations to issue clothing. Many units frowned on the use of such jackets during missions for intelligence reasons.

Opposite page, below: Rations are loaded onto a plane bound for the United States. Two of the crewmen wear the B-10 flight jacket. The AAF stencil is visible on the left shoulder of the jacket of the crewman on the right. The two men at the front, although aircrew, are wearing HBT A-3 mechanic's caps.

Below: Enlisted men enjoy a quiet moment in barracks between missions. Arctic overshoes and service boots are visible underneath the metal bed. At the foot of the bed hangs a B-4 clothing bag, made of cotton duck and reinforced with leather, which was used by some personnel instead of a duffle bag.

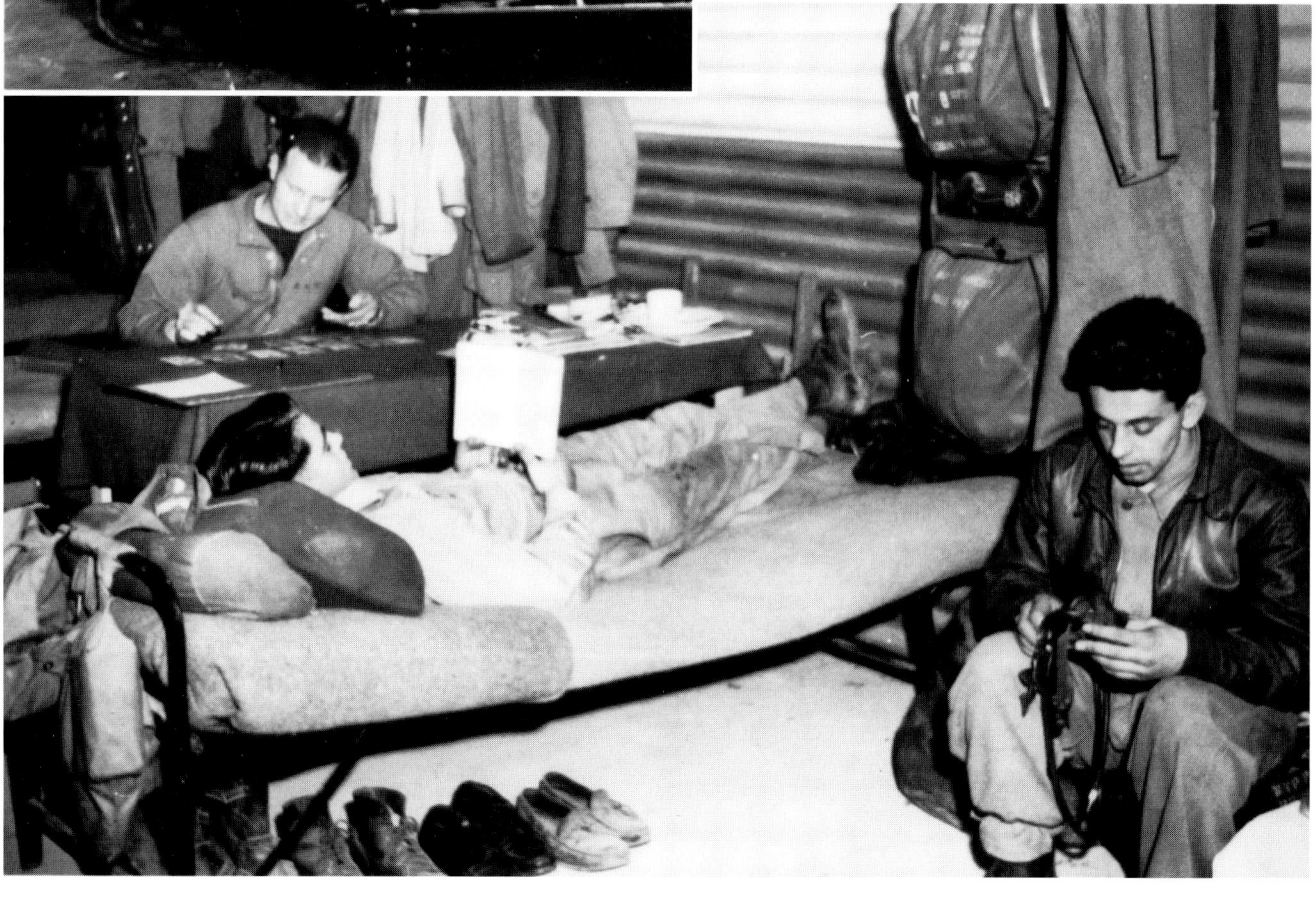

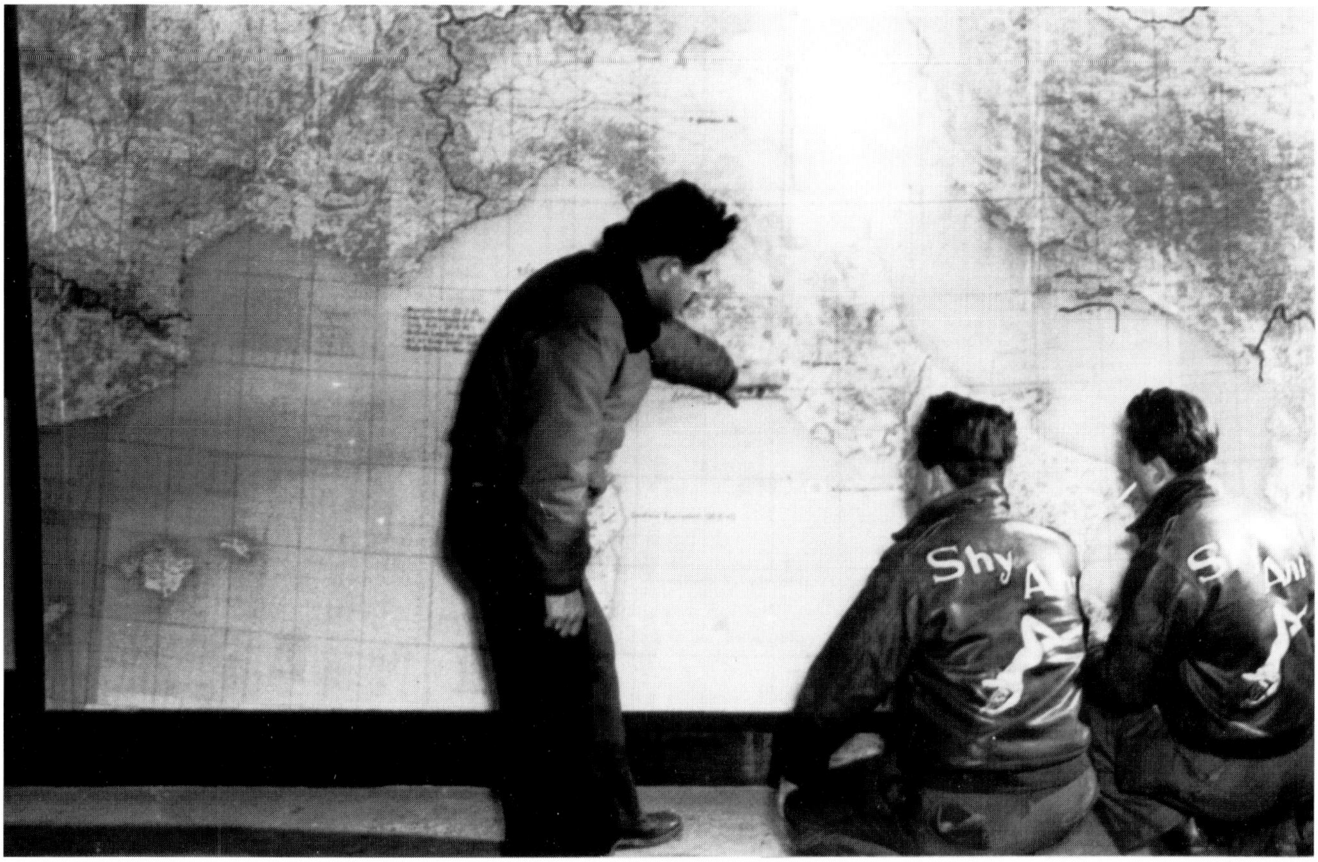
Shy

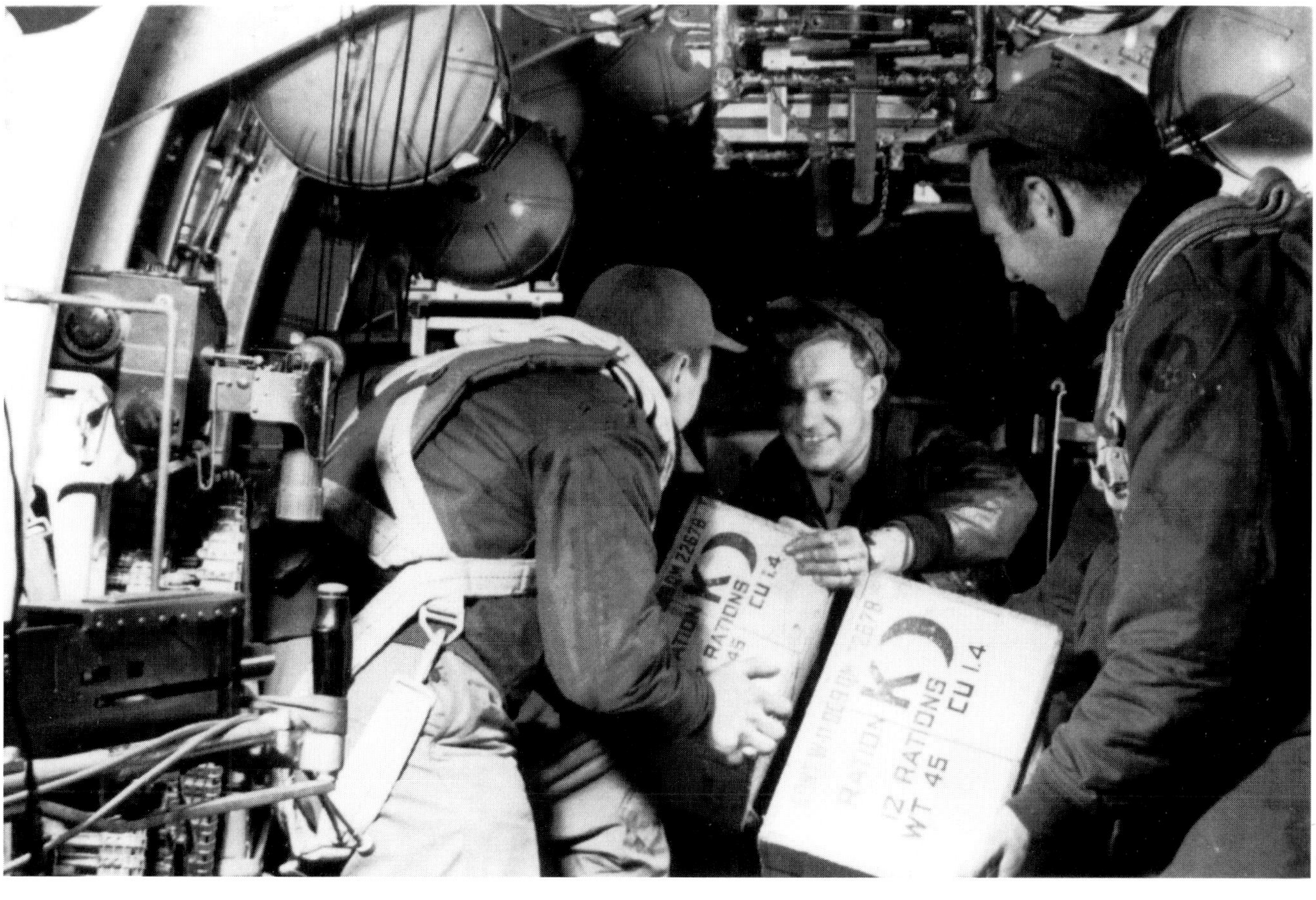
RATION K
12 RATIONS
WT 45
CU 1.4

Opposite page, top: A P-38 'Lightning' is transported down a narrow road after shipment from the United States. One of the greatest logistical feats of the war was the establishment of two American Air Forces in the U.K. Although bombers could make a series of shuttle flights that would get them to Europe, fighters had to be transported across the Atlantic and assembled on arrival, assisted by civilian contractors from the States, as pictured.

Opposite page, bottom: Members of the 401st Bomb Group load supplies into a jeep trailer. Jeeps and their attached trailers were used to transport bomber crews to their aircraft prior to a mission.

Above: Sergeant William Sorrells explains the B-17's oxygen system to ground crew members. Because of the heights at which the bombers operated, crewmembers were required to use their bomber's internal oxygen system. This model oxygen system is set up in front of a mobile shop, which could travel from base to base and provide more advanced training and maintenance work.

Left: An officer examines the contents of a 10-in-one ration. These rations were originally intended to be used by the ground forces and could feed up to ten men. Their weight, however, meant that they were often restricted to vehicle crews. At the end of the war, rations such as these were often dropped by bombers of the Eighth Air Force to the many former Allied prisoners of war awaiting the arrival of advancing ground troops.

Opposite page: A navigator charts his bomber's course. Snapped to his A-11 flight helmet is an A-14 oxygen mask. The A-11 helmet was frequently worn by those crewmembers operating in heated portions of bombers and fighter aircraft. The helmets usually had ANB-H-1 headset receivers placed inside the earpieces and plugged into the plane's intercom system.

Right: A member of the 1199th Military Police Company guards a B-17 of the 303d Bomb Group. This MP is sitting astride an M-1 chain drive solo motorcycle. During the war, Indian and Harley Davidson produced the M-1, which was practical for use on airbases and other rear areas.

Above: Sergeant James Greene crawls from the tail gun position after completing a mission over Frankfurt. The cramped tail-gunner's position in a B-17 could only be reached on hands and knees. In his left hand Greene is carrying a portable oxygen unit, which could be used until the crewman was able to plug himself back in to the ship's internal oxygen system. He has an A-10 mask clipped to his flight helmet.

Opposite page, top: Two members of the Women's Army Corps (WAC) assigned to the Eighth Air Force prepare for a flight. Women did not participate in aerial missions, but were occasionally taken aloft on publicity flights. In addition to their B-3 flight jackets, these women are wearing the WAC winter caps, which were dubbed 'Hobby Hats' after Oveta Culp Hobby, the WAC's first director.

Opposite page, below: Ruby stands beside the B-17 named in her honor. She is wearing the WAC winter overcoat and, curiously, a male garrison cap.

Left: A WAC charts the progress of a mission over Europe. On the left shoulder of her jacket she has sewn the Eighth Air Force insignia. Rather than wear the issue khaki tie, she has chosen to wear a privately purchased knit tie.

Below: The finishing touches are put on the nose art of the B-24 *Pallas Athene: The G.I. Jane.* Athena was the symbol of the WAC and the bust of the Greek goddess appeared on WAC branch of service insignia.

Right: A WAC (right) chats with a British Women's Auxiliary Air Force (WAAF) member. The WAC is wearing the wool winter jacket and skirt with a Hobby hat. This was the standard service uniform of women serving with the Eighth. The jacket and skirt were made of material similar to the male enlisted service uniform.

Below: A column of WACS arrives for duty in England. Since they are arriving in a war zone, these women are all wearing M-1 helmets and carrying their Hobby hats in their hands. The WACS' brown issue utility bag (purse) can be seen on the right hips of these women. WAC purses, which were half-moon shaped, were not the same as those issued to nurses.

Left: A B-17 waist gunner fires on enemy aircraft during a mission. As can be seen in this photograph, the gunner was tethered to his gun position. The variety of wires and cords around him are for his oxygen and intercom. He is wearing the A-4 flight suit over his other flying clothing and a pair of A-6 flight shoes. The early pattern of the A-6 (pictured here) did not have the additional closure straps across the top and ankle that were found on the later A-6A boot.

Opposite page: The navigator of *Bugs* appears relieved to have returned from his latest mission. In his right hand he is carrying a brown leather type A-4 dead reckoning navigation case. In addition to maps and charts, the case contained all of the navigator's special equipment.

Right: A fighter pilot is greeted by his crew chief. Note the crinkly appearance of the mechanic's D-1 shearling jacket. The acrylic varnish that was applied to each jacket after assembly caused the peculiar finish found on all American shearling jackets.

BUGS
THE
GOLDEN-GOPHER

Above: A B-17 bomber crew discusses a recently concluded mission. The man on the far right is wearing the wool knit A-4 mechanic's cap while the man next to him wears the M1941 wool knit 'jeep cap.'

Below: A member of the Eighth waits to be shipped home. The sergeant is wearing the wool ETO jacket, which was favored by many American Army Air Corps members in Europe. News of the surrender of Japan is received in an edition of *Stars and Stripes*, the American serviceman's newspaper.